# Become a Tech-Active Senior

## Defeat Your Fear, Get Connected, Expand Your World

Marie Clapsaddle

ISBN-10: 1533019002
ISBN-13: 978-1533019004

# Dedication

*To Fujiko*

*Thank you for joining me on the journey to a Tech-Active life.*

*Your courage has inspired me to share the joy with other seniors.*

# TABLE OF CONTENTS

# INTRODUCTION

Recently, more and more seniors are discovering the life-enriching benefits of smartphones, computers, tablets, ebook (electronic book) readers, and other devices. As a result, the inaccurate stereotype that all seniors are resistant to technology is beginning to fade. Despite progress, however, too many seniors are reluctant to use these devices.

Some people have already explored with an open mind information about available kinds of tech devices and their benefits, tried one or more, and made an informed decision that they don't want or need them.

Some people have read or heard about these devices but have never tried any of them. They can't fully know what they're missing. If they would read this book and understand the wonderful, life-enriching benefits of these devices, I'm convinced they would want to try them.

So, how about you? Why are you reading this book?

Do you have a tech-timid friend or relative and wish you had a short book to introduce them to the basics? Do you want them to know the many benefits technology has brought into your life? This book will address the reasons people avoid technology and what can be done about it. Please tell them I've been in their shoes and have found answers.

Perhaps this book was given to you by a tech-loving friend or relative, or was recommended to you. Or perhaps you purchased it because you saw more and more people in your social circle using and enjoying tech devices.

Perhaps you have recently found your attitude slowly moving from tech-timid to tech-curious, and you're ready to learn more. You want to see for yourself what it's all about, but something is holding you back.

What is it?

It's the little self-talk voice in your head. It says things like:

"I'm too old."

"I can't do it."

"It's too difficult."

"I don't like it. I don't want it. It's just not for me."

"I'm a klutz—I'd break it."

"I'm embarrassed to ask younger people for help."

"I can't type."

"I'm afraid."

"I can't afford it."

"I feel overwhelmed. I don't know where to start."

The result?

Fear.

I get it. You're not alone.

The little voice in my head has said the same things to me when I've wanted to do something new. Sometimes, I've listened to the voice and given up on my dream. That usually brought regrets. Other times, I confronted the beliefs behind the little voice, proved them false, and felt the fear disappear.

I want to show you how I did it so you can do it, too.

I suspect you've been listening to your little voice and believing it. On top of that, you're not sure what devices might be useful to you or specifically what they can do. You're not sure your life will really be enriched enough to be worth the effort. You worry about the cost involved. And, perhaps most of all you don't know where to begin or how to find support and resources.

Don't despair. This book was written with *you* in mind.

As a senior and a technology enthusiast, I've been interested for a long time in the reasons why seniors are attracted to or repelled by technology. Years ago, I taught myself the basics of computer and Internet use, and eventually became a kind of tech advisor to friends, family, and even coworkers.

As I joined the ranks of those labeled a "senior," I asked other seniors in my social circles their opinions about technology. I even created a short survey to get more opinions from complete strangers. What I learned from all this was surprising, and I can't wait to tell you all about it.

This book is not a manual to teach you how to use a smartphone or computer. There are plenty of books available on such topics, and some of them will be listed in the chapter about resources.

Instead, the gems I hope to share with you focus on:

- overcoming the little voice blocking your path to a richer life

- exploring your options

- learning about the exciting benefits of three types of tech devices

- dealing with the overwhelmed feeling by providing resources

In short, I invite you to join me on a path that has made my life happier and more fulfilled. Many other seniors have taken the same journey and here's what they've told me:

*"My friends and I rely on technology now and learn as we go."*

*"The biggest plus has been to connect with family on Facebook and keep up with what is going on in their lives without having to interrupt their busy schedules. I am glad to have made the transition and I am still walking uphill on the learning curve."*

*"I have a natural curiosity and desire to learn so it was a given that I'd want to explore the benefits of technology. My theory is that those who think this way would be likely to live longer."*

*"When I look back on how frightened I was to use the computer, I feel so silly."*

*"I am not sure how we lived without all these devices before. They are such a huge part of our daily lives and have become more of a need than a luxury item."*

Why am I so confident you can successfully move from tech-timid to tech-curious and on to tech-smart? Because every person I know who has made an open-minded effort to learn about and try one of these devices, using resources like those in this book, has been successful.

Their most common comment is, "Why was I afraid? I never imagined this would change my life in so many wonderful ways. I wish I had started sooner!"

An exciting journey of discovery awaits, and I'm right here to serve as your guide. Life is short, so let's not delay.

# 1. TECH-TIMID?

If you really want to make the move from tech-timid to tech-smart, I have good news for you. The only thing standing in your way is your own mind! How do I know? Because I've seen the evidence in my own life time after time, and also in the lives of others.

It's amazing what you can accomplish with the right attitude and motivation. On the other hand, one thing can stop you in your tracks and guarantee failure. What is it? The little voice in your head that spews negative self-talk. It talks you out of your dreams and prevents you from taking even the first step. Then, it berates you later with, "See, you're hopeless. You can't do anything. Everybody else is smarter, more skillful than you."

The little voice means well. It's trying to protect you, keep you from taking risks, and prevent physical or emotional pain. The sad thing is that the little voice's advice and cautions are based on fear, and the fear is based on unquestioned false beliefs.

We are embarking on the exciting journey that will help you become a tech-curious learner and then a tech-smart device user.

The first step is to clear the roadblocks created by your little voice. I'll help you examine the false information the little voice has been feeding you, and you'll be able to master your feelings and beliefs. A wonderful side benefit of this process is that you'll be able to apply what you learn here to other areas of your life.

So, a friend or relative tries to tell you how great it is to use a computer, smartphone, or some other electronic device. Or, you see television shows or advertisements depicting people happily using such devices. For a fleeting moment, you sense a tiny flame of desire to experience this lifestyle for yourself, but the desire is immediately squelched by a gripping sense of fear. You let the fear win without ever questioning it.

Let's take a deeper look at the fear and what is causing it.

Whenever you fear something, chances are the feeling comes immediately after listening to the little voice in your head. Sadly, the little voice's comments are almost always negative and based on unquestioned beliefs.

The good news is that beliefs can be confronted, and when they're examined objectively a more balanced view can be achieved. In this process, your mind sees the truth of the matter and the negative, untrue belief automatically loses its power over you. A sense of empowerment replaces the fear, and you can take control of your own decision-making process.

I've collected a list of the most common self-talk roadblocks related to our journey. Let's examine them one by one, and see them dissolve.

## I'm too old.

This is one of the most common false beliefs among seniors and one of the most irrational. It's based on a stereotype founded on ignorance. Seniors who have refused to let society's stereotypes hold them back often say, "Age is just a number." They ignore the stereotype as the lie it truly is, and go on to enjoy a fulfilled life.

Look around you. Do you see others in your social circle and those much older than you enjoying technology? They're obviously not "too old" so why should you be?

You can choose to let yourself be labeled by a false stereotype, or you can be one more person to prove it wrong. Which will it be? It's your choice.

## I can't do it.

How do you know? Have you tried it? Are you accepting this false belief based on some other thing you tried and failed to master? If so, keep in mind that failure in one area does not automatically mean failure in another.

As you face this new challenge, you're older and you've had more life experience. On top of that, isn't it possible the earlier failure might have been a success if you had just kept trying a bit longer? The earlier failure could have been caused by a lack of guidance or resources, and that won't be a problem this time.

When my little voice tries to feed me this lie, I question: "Can't, or won't?" That puts it into perspective, and then I have to face the truth. The problem isn't inability. It's refusal to try. And, the refusal is usually based on irrational fear.

# It's too difficult.

Next, the little voice will use the argument, "It's too difficult."

Huh? Wait a minute. You aren't going to just accept that without examining it, are you? Think about it. How does one objectively measure "too difficult"? Difficult is a relative term, and those of us with low self-confidence often sell ourselves short before we even try something new.

I can think of numerous examples of learning some new skill. At first it seemed overwhelming and scary. Then, after a short time, it became familiar. At that point, I looked back on my unfounded fear and thought, "That wasn't so bad after all. In fact, it was much easier than I expected." Before long, I was not only comfortable with the new skill, but I was teaching it to others!

Take one common example in your own life. Have you learned how to drive a car? Do you remember how scary it was the first time you tried it? You were fearful that you would never be able to master the steering, clutch, shifting, braking, monitoring the mirrors, and evaluating traffic conditions all at the same time.

After years of driving, you look back at your earlier self and laugh at the fears. In fact, driving is so easy and natural that you occasionally don't even remember parts of your trip because your brain is operating on a kind of "autopilot."

This is just one example proving the point that any new challenge will always seem "too difficult." If you have never needed to drive a car, then substitute the experience of learning to ride a bicycle or some similar skill.

The only way to defeat the "too difficult" lie is to take the first step and not let yourself quit before you give the new skill a chance.

One more thing about the "It's too difficult" excuse. Consider the possibility that even if the challenge you face really is extremely difficult and will require great courage, it's likely the benefits will far outweigh the difficulty. I've seen this to be true with technology.

## I'm embarrassed to ask for help from younger people.

Why are you embarrassed? What is the shame in learning something from another person, no matter what their age? Are you concerned your need for help will be an annoyance to them? Do you fear asking for help somehow makes you look dependent and weak or less intelligent?

I think false beliefs are again coloring your feelings and decisions. I like to think of the teaching and learning process as one of mutual benefit.

During my years as a teacher, my thoughts were focused on how enjoyable it was to share something important to me with someone who wanted this information. I never considered that my students were somehow beneath me just because I knew things they didn't know. Based on years of experience and observation, I've found people are pleased if you ask them to teach you something—especially if it's something about which they are passionate.

If the older/younger issue is still a barrier, try thinking of it in another way. As an older person, you have spent years teaching and helping others. Isn't it only fair that you give younger people a chance to reciprocate? By resisting, you're denying them an opportunity to feel the sense of satisfaction and fulfillment that comes with sharing their knowledge and helping someone else.

Not only that, but such an arrangement frequently results in an intergenerational friendship that enriches both people. Then, there are opportunities for you to reciprocate by sharing with your younger tech helper from your greater wealth of experience and wisdom.

Don't let false pride hold you back from benefits you would never have imagined.

# I'm a klutz—I'd break it.

Most of us faced this fear the first time we sat down at a computer. We thought pressing the wrong key would cause the computer to blow up or erase all the contents. We had an unrealistic image of how a computer worked and what was safe or unsafe.

As knowledge and experience increased, we quickly realized our mental image was totally wrong and silly. Also, we learned almost any mistake can be easily corrected. With increased knowledge came increased confidence.

Fortunately, today we have smartphones and tablets, devices that are smaller and less intimidating, yet capable of doing almost everything a computer can do. Like a computer, any fear of damaging them through use is simply the normal fear of anything new and unfamiliar. It will pass with a little experience.

Even if the fear is about physically damaging the device by some accident such as dropping it, there are solutions like breakage insurance, protective cases, and screen protector sheets.

# I'm afraid.

This is perhaps the most difficult barrier to overcome. It's an irrational, baseless fear you can't explain or justify—even to yourself. It's formless and defies your attempts to combat it.

I like to think of it as merely fear of the unknown. It's the general sense of fear that washes over you when facing a new challenge of any kind. You don't know what steps to take, what problems may arise, or if you'll be successful.

Your little voice will try to keep you in your familiar comfort zone by telling you the risks are too great. It will present images of all the worst possible things that could happen and tell you that you're going to fail for sure.

I realize the little voice is just doing its job of trying to protect you. However, when its attempts to protect end up smothering you and preventing you from enjoying life to the fullest, it's time to tell the little voice who's boss.

Here are the facts the little voice doesn't seem to want you to know:

- Most fears are based on false information, incorrect beliefs, or wrong interpretations.

- The majority of the things you fear never happen.

- Even when something does go wrong, it's almost never as bad as you imagined.

- In fact, the outcomes are often way *better* than you imagined.

So, just tell the little voice, "You're not the boss of me!"

# I don't like it. I don't want it. It's not for me.

My first question is, "Have you tried it?" If you have given it a fair chance, I respect your decision.

I went through this with microwave ovens. At first I feared and distrusted them. As they became more common and accessible, I tried one at my workplace lunch room. I could see they had some benefits of convenience and saving time. On the other hand, I weighed the cost-benefit ratio for someone like me who would only use it occasionally. I also read reports claiming the process of cooking with microwaves might reduce the nutritional quality of foods. I noted a microwave oven would take up at least half of my meager counter space. In the end, I decided I didn't want a microwave oven because it wasn't a good match for my lifestyle.

Maybe you tried a computer or some other tech device a long time ago, decided you didn't like it, and haven't touched one since then. In the field of technology, things change in a big way in only a few years. Something that may have been unpleasant or difficult for you several years ago may have been redesigned or changed in some way that eliminates the negative issues you remember. It might be worth investigating whether your original decision is still the best decision for you.

If you haven't tried a computer or other device, your belief that it isn't for you is just an assumption based on no evidence. How many times have you heard of a child refusing some vegetable despite parental coaxing? Maybe one of your current favorite foods used to be one you thought you hated as a child.

I grew up far from a sea coast and the only kind of fish served in my home was frozen fish sticks. I could barely tolerate fish in this form and totally rejected anything with a stronger "fishy" taste. When I grew older, I heard about sushi and avoided trying it because I thought surely raw fish would be slimy and smelly. I thought my beliefs were supported by reasonable assumptions, but I had never tried raw fish.

Flash forward to my move to Japan as an English teacher. By this time, I had convinced myself the only way to survive and thrive in a new culture was to unquestioningly try anything once before deciding whether or not I liked it. With this new frame of mind, I hesitantly tried sushi and discovered my assumptions were completely wrong.

Sushi became one of my favorite Japanese foods. I learned an important lesson: Never prejudge and reject something until you have honestly given it a chance.

# I can't type.

Don't let inability to type stop you. I know plenty of people who get along just fine on a computer keyboard with two-finger "hunt and peck" typing for the small amount of typing they need to do. Unless you plan to write a book or create many long documents, you may find yourself using the mouse or trackpad more than the keyboard. If touch typing really is a necessity, there are free courses available on the Internet that will teach you typing.

Chances are you may find a smartphone or tablet to be more suitable than a computer. The on-screen keyboard of these devices is too small for the kind of touch typing possible on a physical keyboard anyway. The on-screen keyboard adapts to your input and suggests words as you type, making your input faster and easier. Also, some on-screen keyboards have a swipe feature, allowing you to type by swiping your finger from one letter to the next.

With smartphones and tablets, you have one more helpful feature. It's possible to input your information by speaking the sentences. How amazing it is to see your words appearing on the screen as you talk, as if by magic!

# I'm worried about the money.

Perhaps you're beginning to think you're ready to explore the world of the tech-curious. But just as you start to have hope, the little voice reasserts itself with negative thoughts like, "You can't afford it" or "You'll waste your money. You'll buy one of these devices and then never use it."

As usual, the little voice doesn't have all the facts and is just pushing whatever negative thoughts will make you stay stuck in your risk-free comfort zone.

Here are some facts you may not have considered.

There are several ways to get an Internet connection in your home, and the types of plans and prices vary widely. Special offers are available for new customers, and discounts exist for people with low incomes (usually through some kind of government program). These days, having an Internet connection is seen more and more as a necessity rather than a luxury.

Devices are available from many manufacturers in a wide range of prices, and refurbished or used devices are available at a big cost saving. Also, it's possible someone in your own family or circle of friends has a device they no longer need that might be available for a bargain price or even free. Once they become aware of your interest, you never know what opportunities may appear.

Don't be concerned about a device going unused; this rarely happens. When you invest money in an item, you are motivated to use it, and your willingness to learn will inspire others around you to offer their help. Possession of the new device with a desire to learn is the ticket granting you entrance into the tech-curious world.

## I want to start but I'm overwhelmed and don't know where to begin.

Perfect. That's a normal reaction when faced with a completely new learning opportunity. We all feel like this at the beginning.

The feeling of paralysis comes from not having information in small, clear steps. It also comes from a feeling of being all alone, facing the new challenge without support from a guide or mentor.

One purpose of this book is to provide basic information about the main categories of tech devices that might interest you, and to explain their benefits. The other purpose is to suggest resources to get you started on your new journey.

# You're the boss!

I love the quote from William James: "The greatest discovery of any generation is that a human being can alter his life by altering his attitude."

You've come a long way already. Together, we have faced the negative self-talk of the little voice and considered counterarguments.

You're beginning to see that the little voice has been keeping you stuck in your tech-timid comfort zone. It used to feel safe and cozy in there, but now it's beginning to look more like a prison cell, keeping you away from the wonderful tech-curious world outside.

The good news is that *you* are the one holding the key to the cell door, and you can open it if you choose. The key is the truth—the truth that comes from receiving new facts and rethinking your old beliefs.

It's time to choose a new attitude, open up the cell door, and boldly step out into the tech-curious world. New friends and opportunities await you.

The key is in your hand. Do it now.

# 2. WHICH DEVICE IS FOR ME?

There are plenty of good books available in bookstores and through the Internet that can help you learn how to use a tech device. Rather, my purpose is to give you an introduction to the most commonly used types of devices and provide an overview of what they can do. This will help you decide where to start and what devices might be useful to you.

I'll introduce smartphones, computers and tablets, and e-readers (electronic book readers) below and then explain each in more depth in later chapters.

You may feel overwhelmed at all the things these devices can do, but please keep in mind that you don't have to learn and use every feature of a device. You can pick and choose, focusing only on the features of interest to you.

# SMARTPHONE

A smartphone is a portable phone with computer-like capabilities, but it's operated with a touchscreen rather than a keyboard. It can make calls, send text messages, and access the Internet through applications (called "apps" for short) including a browser.

If you're taking your first step into the tech-curious world, a smartphone is a great place to start. They can do many of the same things as computers, but they're easier to learn, more portable, and less expensive.

Let's take a look at some of the benefits of a smartphone.

## A smartphone can replace your landline phone.

Ever since mobile phones started to become popular, more and more people have decided having a landline seems unnecessary. By getting rid of their landline, they cut down on monthly expenses, and they don't have to deal with two phone numbers. As smartphones entered the mobile phone market, this trend has increased.

# A smartphone is convenient.

Years ago, pay phones used to be conveniently located almost everywhere. Today, locating a pay phone when needed is difficult if not impossible. Besides, is it likely you would have the necessary coins on hand to make a call? These days, people carry little cash, much less coins. Smartphones have mostly replaced pay phones. People depend on their smartphone to notify their friends when they're running late. Calls can be made and received from anywhere including inside a car.

# A smartphone promotes safety and peace of mind.

People who carry a smartphone feel more comfortable traveling alone, especially at night. They know they can call police, ambulance, road assistance, a friend, or a family member immediately from wherever they are.

# A smartphone is useful for people with difficulty hearing.

It's easy to adjust the volume on a smartphone. Also, some kind of plug-in headset with microphone can be used, channeling the sound directly into your ears. This helps block out background noise and makes it easier to carry on a phone conversation or listen to music.

## A smartphone can replace a camera.

Not so long ago, people used to carry around a camera if they wanted to capture photos of scenery, special events, or vacation locations. Film was expensive and the number of possible exposures was limited. Added to the cost of the camera and film was developing and printing of photographs. Having to take or send the film somewhere and wait to receive the finished photos was inconvenient.

Smartphones have largely replaced point-and-shoot cameras for the average person. A smartphone, with its built-in camera, allows anyone to capture a photo or video anytime and anywhere. The number of photos possible is practically unlimited. Photos can be reviewed on the spot and unwanted shots deleted. The best photos can be stored on the phone and shown off to friends, or shared with others without the cost of printing. It's possible to make prints on one's home color printer, or at a local drugstore or Big Box store like Walmart.

# COMPUTER

Computers are available in desktop, notebook, and tablet form.

Desktops and notebooks are powerful machines for both personal and business use. Among the most used features of computers are email (electronic mail), calendar, contacts (an address book), and the browser.

With the browser a search can be done for topics (to be covered in more detail in a later chapter) such as research, shopping, education, news, banking, entertainment, sports, social, hobbies and interests, spiritual support, and information useful to seniors and people that are housebound or disabled.

Other computer features people enjoy are the photo library, music library, live video chat, and productivity programs.

Tablets are much like giant smartphones without the ability to make calls. Like smartphones, they have a touch-sensitive screen and don't require a physical keyboard. They're convenient to use anywhere, and generally cost less than a computer or high-end smartphone. In most cases they're not as powerful or flexible as a computer, so they're more suited to simple tasks such as email and watching videos rather than professional photo editing or business applications such as writing long documents or working with spreadsheets.

# E-READER

Perhaps you are saying to yourself, "I have access to print books from the local bookstore and the library. Why should I want to read ebooks on an e-reader?"

I've been a lover of books and reading since I was a child, so I understand the feelings of those who might ask this question. I used to feel the same way. However, shipping boxes of books in international and cross-country moves, facing small apartments with shrinking storage space, living in locations without a useful library, and experiencing the continually rising cost of print books were just a few things that made me want to find out more about ebooks.

I discovered ebooks could solve many of the problems I was experiencing while yielding benefits I hadn't even imagined. I also came to realize that embracing electronic reading didn't mean I had to completely abandon my beloved print books. I could have the best of both worlds.

In the end, I got rid of most of my print books by selling them to used bookstores, giving them to friends, or donating them to the local library. I kept those with special sentimental value, and those that would be difficult to replace or use in ebook format.

Now that I've retained only the print books with special meaning, and ones I intend to read again in the future, my small collection takes up only two narrow shelves. I realized the majority of books people keep on their bulging bookshelves or stored away in boxes in the basement are not easily accessible and will likely never be reread. They will become dusty, musty, or water damaged, and will become a burden in the event of a move or downsizing.

Lovers of travel should definitely try an e-reader. People who travel with print books have to deal with the extra weight, the inability to bring all the books they would like to have available, and the hassle of what to do with books they finish reading during their trip. An e-reader with built-in light makes it easy to read in a darkened plane, and an e-reader/tablet also provides music and video options in one compact package.

E-reader devices generally accept only ebook formats compatible with their brand. In this book, I'm going to focus on Amazon Kindle ebooks and the two types of e-readers produced by Amazon. I made this choice because Amazon is the largest and most popular source of ebooks and reading devices.

Apple iBooks, a competitor to Amazon Kindle ebooks, deserve at least a mention. Apple does not produce any e-reader devices, but their iBooks can be read and purchased through the iBooks app on an iPhone or iPad. The disadvantage of iBooks is that they can only be read on an Apple device, whereas Amazon Kindle ebooks can be read on Amazon e-reader devices, Apple and Android mobile devices (through the free Kindle Reader apps), and on Windows or Apple computers. This cross-platform capability is a huge advantage of Amazon ebooks.

Amazon produces two types of e-readers in various models and price points. One type is the dedicated Kindle line (used only for reading ebooks) with "e-ink" technology that makes the black-and-white screen look like print on paper. The other type is the line of Fire Tablet devices with color screens. Fire Tablets have the same capabilities as other tablet devices such as installing apps, and playing videos, music, and audiobooks.

Fans of ebook reading usually report they were won over by the portability and capacity of e-readers. They love carrying around hundreds of books in one lightweight device the size of a paperback book.

Ebooks solve the problem of lack of storage and display space. Bedtime readers enjoy having multiple books at their fingertips instead of dealing with a stack of print books on the nightstand.

Ebooks make reading several books at the same time easier because they automatically remember the point where the reader stopped.

The ability to adjust an ebook's font size and style, margins, and line spacing make reading a customized experience not possible with a print book.

People who choose to purchase a Fire Tablet or a Kindle device with the built-in light can enjoy reading in the dark anywhere. This is especially useful for reading in bed or while traveling.

Although there are some exceptions, the ebook version of a book is usually cheaper than its print counterpart and these days some books are available only in ebook form.

Ebooks purchased from Amazon are stored in the Kindle Library under the customer's account. Users can put a copy of any ebooks from this library on their e-reader and then delete the copy when they finish reading the book. This means they can have as many or as few ebooks on their device as they choose.

Readers of ebooks save money. While the big publishers frequently price their ebooks at $9.99 or above, a large number of ebooks from other sources sell for under $4.00, with some as low as $0.99, and many for free. Amazon sells ebooks from the big-name publishers, from self-published authors, and also a good selection of public domain ebooks and classics.

I hope this overview has sparked an interest to learn more about tech devices. The following chapters will explore these in more detail, starting with smartphones.

# 3. SMARTPHONES

Not surprisingly, seniors frequently choose a smartphone as their first tech device. Smartphones are among the most versatile and useful tech devices available today.

Smartphones come in many sizes, designs, and price ranges. The two most used operating systems are Apple iOS and Android. Both have advantages and disadvantages, so choosing one over the other is mostly a matter of personal preference.

Smartphones are made by multiple companies including Samsung, Google, HTC, Sony, and Apple. They're sold in small stores operated by the main carriers such as AT&T, Verizon, Sprint, and T-Mobile. They're also available through companies offering discounted service plans.

Some examples of carriers offering cheap plans are Net10, Cricket, Red Pocket, Simple Mobile,

Straight Talk, and Republic Wireless. Bargain phones with discount plans are also available in Big Box stores like Walmart and Best Buy.

In addition to price and features, one of the most important considerations in choosing a smartphone is whether the carrier has good call reception in your location. If you live in a rural area, be sure to ask people around you for their carrier recommendations.

Inexpensive "prepaid" smartphones like TracFone are sold at Big Box stores and even at supermarkets. Prepaid phone users buy an activation card for the amount of service that suits their budget and needs, thus, avoiding a long-term carrier contract.

Next, let's take a look at the key smartphone features (calling, contacts, text messages, calendar, email, the browser, the camera, and apps) and explain what they are and how they're useful.

## Calling

As might be expected, one of the most common uses of a smartphone is making and receiving phone calls. As we already noted, the ability to call anytime, anywhere is what sets a mobile phone apart from a landline or pay phone.

Smartphones have settings for customization such as replacing the loud ringing sound with a vibration when quiet is necessary. Other settings allow the ringing to be silenced during sleeping hours, and callers can leave a voice message to be checked later.

## Contacts

Another side benefit of smartphone calling is the integrated contacts list. From here, commonly used phone numbers can be called quickly and easily. There's also the option to include a contact's email address, mailing address, and personal notes such as birthdays. Having all this information in an easily editable form is an advantage over paper address books.

## Text Messages

Text messages are short messages sent directly from one phone to another. They appear immediately on the recipient's phone but can be answered when convenient. Text messages are gradually winning out over calling (especially with the younger generation). Text messages are quick, convenient, effective, and often included free with phone contracts.

# Calendar

In the same way phone contacts are replacing paper address books, the smartphone calendar feature offers an alternative to paper calendars. Since the smartphone is always close at hand, it seems like the best place to keep a record of appointments and recurring events requiring a reminder. Smartphone calendars use the notification feature to send a one-time or recurring reminder by a screen message and notification sound.

# Email

Like a computer, smartphones send and receive email. With its much smaller screen and lack of a physical keyboard, email on a smartphone isn't as pleasant as on a computer. Still, it's convenient to know there's incoming email and to be able to quickly check the contents.

One way that smartphone email shines is the ability to take a photo directly from the phone, attach it to an email, and send it to anyone. In the same way, photos attached to incoming emails can be saved on the recipient's phone.

Email has multiple benefits. It's faster and cheaper than a letter. As with a text message, the recipient isn't interrupted with a ringing phone demanding immediate attention, but email is better suited for longer messages than texts.

People living in different time zones especially value email because it's so difficult to arrange a good time for a call.

Photos and other attachments can be sent with an email, and information is easily forwarded in an email with a URL link. (More about URLs in Chapter 4.)

Three widely used email services are: Yahoo! Mail (www.yahoo.com), Gmail (www.gmail.com), and Hotmail (www.hotmail.com). It's easy to set up an account on any one of them.

Perhaps you don't think email would be useful to you. Maybe you're thinking, "Who would I send email to?"

A few years ago, Fujiko, a senior friend of mine in Japan had the same reservations. I assured her that once she had an email account, she would discover all kinds of unexpected uses.

Fujiko had little tech experience except inserting a tape into her TV video recorder and pressing the record button. She believed learning how to program the video recorder was beyond her abilities, so the mere thought of buying a computer and learning how to use email made her fearful.

Still, she observed how much fun I was having with email. She saw how I was able to avoid expensive long-distance calls and still keep in touch with family and friends back in the U.S. She marveled that I could send an email and receive a reply in hours rather than the ten days required for postal mail.

Finally, I persuaded Fujiko to try exchanging email with me (even though we lived in the same city and talked frequently on the phone). I helped her choose a small notebook computer and set up an email account. I wrote down step-by-step instructions, and we practiced these steps until she was comfortable. After that, we exchanged email messages several times a week.

Fujiko started telling friends about her computer and email experiences, laughing about the fact that she had only one person in her contacts. Before long, a few friends started using email and her contacts began to grow.

She began sending email to a long-time American friend and a sister-in-law, both living in the U.S. Then, she met a visitor from New Zealand and was excited that she could keep in touch with her by email after she returned to her country.

Before long, Fujiko reported she was sending regular emails to some students she had taught in Sunday School decades earlier. Recently, she told me she has 25 people in her contacts. Of course, now that I've returned to the U.S., email is the main way Fujiko and I keep in touch.

Like Fujiko, you'll find plenty of friends and family to add to your email contacts.

Besides personal use, email is also convenient for contacting businesses or government agencies. Some businesses send news or information about special sales through an email list. For example, my local supermarket sends a weekly specials flyer by email.

You can see now why I think email is one of the most useful features of a smartphone or computer.

# Browser

A browser is a window on the screen that gives access to the Internet. Using Google Search or other similar services in the browser, searches for all kinds of information are possible.

There are Internet websites devoted to hobbies, finances, history, politics, religion, news, science, shopping, entertainment, and technology, to name just a few. The browser is also the doorway to accessing educational sites offering free courses on all kinds of subjects.

# Camera

In addition to taking photos, a smartphone camera can record videos. Also, live video chatting through a service like Skype is a wonderful way to stay in touch with distant friends, children, or grandchildren. Video calls are almost as good as being there in person.

# Apps

"App" is an abbreviation for "application." Apps are small software programs available from an Internet store right on the phone. Each app is represented on the screen by an "icon" (a small colorful symbol you touch to open and use the app).

Every smartphone comes with some basic apps pre-installed and one of these is the Google "Play Store" (for Android phones) or the Apple "App Store" (for iPhone users). These are the gateway to the store where free or inexpensive apps can be added to the phone.

Now, let's take a look at a few of the most popular kinds of apps to give you an idea of what is available.

# Weather

Before the days of smartphones, people used to get a weather report once daily from the radio or television. Now, smartphones with weather apps display current weather conditions, weekly/daily/hourly forecasts, weather warnings, and weather maps for any city. It's a great way to keep informed about local weather, the situation where loved ones live, and conditions at a vacation destination.

# Games

App stores are full of games. Some are played alone, and others can be played turn by turn with one or more participants even at a distance. For example, there are arcade-style games (Cut the Rope, Candy Crush Saga and Angry Birds), versions of board games (The Game of Life, Monopoly, Scrabble, Chess, Dominos, Mahjong, and Cribbage), card games (Solitaire, Hearts, Spades, Lotto, Rummy, Pitch, and Uno), puzzle games (Plants vs. Zombies, Tetris, Jenga, Cascade, Crossword, Word Search, Sudoku, and Bejeweled), trivia games (Wheel of Fortune, Trivia Crack, Family Feud, and Jeopardy), and many more.

# Photo Editing

Photo editing brings out the best in your pictures. With photo editing apps, you can adjust the brightness or color balance, crop the size, rotate the photo, add captions, and add filters to change the mood.

# Instagram

The Instagram app is the gateway to a social site where photography fans share their photos with others. Members leave comments under photos, creating a sense of community.

# Music

If you already have a computer with digital music purchased from the Internet or transferred from a CD, some or all can be copied to your smartphone. Having your own music on your phone allows you to enjoy the specific music you want to hear without worrying about using data from your phone contract monthly data allowance.

If you have chosen a generous data plan or don't have your own music, you might choose a streaming music subscription such as Spotify or Apple Music instead for about $10 per month.

Some apps like Pandora allow you to choose favorite genres of music and then play random music from those categories. Apps like this usually have a free option that may include occasional advertisements, and an ad-free subscription option with some extra features.

TuneIn Radio provides access to some local radio stations from all over the world, and this means you can also enjoy talk radio in addition to music. It also gives you access to some podcasts (details below) and audiobooks, news, and sports.

One added benefit of listening to music on a smartphone is that earphones improve your ability to hear clearly without bothering people around you.

## Streaming Video

Smartphones bring all kinds of entertainment right to the palm of your hand. Today's smartphones are available with large high-resolution screens making videos more enjoyable to watch. Also, as with music, wearing earphones can improve your listening experience.

The YouTube app is being used more and more by people of all ages in recent years because it provides free content as well as a new subscription service. On YouTube, you can find movie trailers, movies and documentaries, music, comedy, product reviews, and how-to videos, just to name a few.

These days, people are saving money by dropping their cable television subscription and substituting Internet content viewed on a computer, smartphone, or tablet.

In addition to YouTube, some television networks have apps that allow viewing of selected content on smartphones. Also, streaming video apps from Amazon, Apple, and Google bring access to individual TV series episodes and movies. The Hulu app has free and paid TV series content. Netflix has movies and TV episodes viewable through flat-rate monthly plans.

## Languages

If you enjoy foreign travel, a translation app might be of interest. Some require typed input, and others, such as Google's Translate app, also let you speak the words and the smartphone speaks back the translation.

## Maps

The Maps app is another useful app whether at home or on vacation. It helps you find locations and directions for how to get there, complete with turn-by-turn instructions.

## Podcasts

Podcasts have been around for years but it seems few people are familiar with them. Podcasts are digital audio or video files made available on the Internet for downloading to a computer, smartphone, or tablet, usually received automatically by subscription.

The term "subscription" often confuses those unfamiliar with podcasts, since most podcasts are free and the term just means you indicate to the podcast app that you want to automatically receive each new episode of a podcast.

Podcasts are available about topics like news, politics, technology, music, science, comedy, how-to, business, finances, health, social issues, culture, sports, education, games and hobbies, and religion/spirituality. Some public radio networks make their programs available in podcast form so they can be received and enjoyed according to the listener's schedule.

Several years ago just before Christmas, I was hit by a car while crossing an intersection. I ended up in the hospital for surgery on my leg. As it turned out, I had to spend more than a week in the hospital.

I had no family nearby, and all my friends and coworkers were occupied with holiday preparations, so visitors were rare. Television wasn't readily available, and it held little interest for me anyway. I wasn't in the mood to focus on reading which was just as well since there was little suitable reading material to be had.

If I hadn't had access to a daily replenishing supply of interesting podcasts to keep me company, block out the worry, and pass the time, I don't know how I would have endured that experience. Podcasts are still an important part of my daily life, providing entertainment and mental stimulation.

## Social Media

We have already discussed the Instagram app, an example of a social media app centered around sharing photos. Three more social sites of note are Facebook, Twitter, and Pinterest.

Facebook helps people reestablish contact with school classmates and keep in touch with friends and family by brief posts and photos. With proper privacy settings, these are viewable only by people in their "friends list." Facebook makes it easy to share information with multiple people at no cost.

Twitter helps individuals and businesses make connections. Anyone can create a free Twitter account and "follow" other Twitter users. Those you follow may choose to also follow you, or not. You see all the messages written by everyone you follow, and private direct messages can also be sent between people that follow each other. Twitter posts are limited to 140 characters, so it's fairly easy to keep up with posts from a large number of people. Individuals and companies appreciate Twitter as a convenient means of communication and promotion.

Pinterest allows users to save and share favorite photos or images they see around the Internet by "pinning" them to "boards." Examples of board topics are travel locations, recipe ideas, fashion hints, home decorating ideas, and items to be purchased. A topic search on Pinterest will bring up all sorts of interesting ideas.

## Messaging apps

Messaging apps accomplish the same purpose as the built-in text message feature on a smartphone but have some advantages. With a messaging app, knowledge of the other person's email address or phone number is not necessary.

Some phone carrier plans charge a per-message fee or do not make texting available at all. In this case, messaging apps offer a free alternative to text messages.

Google Hangouts, WhatsApp, Telegram, and LINE are examples of messaging apps used by people all over the world. Facebook also has their own app, appropriately named "Messenger."

Recently, some messaging apps have started offering the ability to make free voice calls to people on your app's contact list. This is a nice alternative if you're running short on minutes available with your phone contract and don't mind using some data to make a call.

One of my favorite smartphone apps is the LINE messaging app. I use it to keep in touch with my sister who lives at a distance. Multiple times each day, we exchange photos and brief messages about our activities. With special features built into the LINE app, we can add stickers (humorous cartoon pictures) or emoji (small pictorial symbols such as smiley faces) to our messages, or add filters to customize the appearance of our photos. I send her photos of my latest knitting projects. She sends me vacation photos and shots of the latest antics of her two cats.

Messaging apps are great fun and a wonderful way to stay in touch with friends and family.

# News

There are many ways to access news with smartphone apps. Some of the big TV networks produce their own news app. Other apps like Flipboard present contents from a variety of sources in a magazine-like format. For those who want only highlights or breaking news, CNN, NBC and others have created Breaking News apps.

The Twitter app mentioned above is another way to receive news from anywhere in the world. You can follow accounts that post information about breaking news, political news, natural disasters, celebrity activities, notices from local government offices, utility outages, shopping bargains, and more.

There are some advantages to using Twitter as a source of news. You choose the sources and types of news you receive, and the reports are brief and timely. Also, it's possible to follow the accounts of individuals present at the scene of the news. This provides a balance to the perspectives presented by network news channels by giving you first-hand observations and opinions of the "man on the street."

# Sports

Sports apps abound for every kind of sport and all the major teams. Apps have also been created to help athletes train by viewing instructions and techniques, and recording their repetitions, times, speed, and other stats. If you already have cable or other similar access to games and want to view while on the go, there are apps that allow you to verify your cable account and view games on your smartphone or tablet.

# Banking

Today it's less necessary to make trips to the bank than in the past. People have their paycheck or Social Security payment automatically deposited into their bank account, and they pay for goods and services with a credit or debit card. However, there's still the occasional situation when they receive a check in the mail or need to transfer money between their checking and savings account.

Now that more and more people have a computer or smartphone, almost all banking business can be done without leaving home. This is a real convenience for any busy person, but it's especially a bonus for seniors, those who are housebound, the disabled, or anyone who has transportation problems.

With a smartphone app provided by your bank, it's possible to transfer money between accounts, check balances, and schedule payments. You can even deposit a check by signing it and using the app's camera feature to photograph the front and back of the check—all from the comfort of your home.

## Shopping

People who have access to the Internet can buy just about anything they need without leaving the house, often cheaper than at brick-and-mortar stores, and with free shipping.

Of course, the shopping experience is much more enjoyable on a big computer screen, but it's also possible on a smartphone—especially one of the larger models. Smartphone screens can be "zoomed" to temporarily make a part of the screen contents larger and easier to read. Also, many companies have made their website auto-adapt to smartphone screens, changing its configuration to be easier to read and better suited to touch interaction.

Some stores and businesses have created their own app. From the largest retailers like Amazon, to national chains like pizza delivery companies, to local businesses there are apps. In addition to browsing offerings and buying things, these apps may give customers extra perks such as coupons, discount codes, and bonus points for future discounts.

Did you ever wish you could receive a personal notification from your favorite store when items on your shopping list went on sale? Believe it or not, there are apps for that.

One example, PriceRadar, links to your Amazon wish list with settings to indicate the percentage or dollar amount of the price drop at which you want to be notified. The app checks the list periodically, sending a screen notification when a price drop is detected.

Do you ever get annoyed at all those little barcoded loyalty cards hanging off your keychain? Good news! There are apps that let you put the loyalty card information on your smartphone. The store clerk can scan the barcode right from your phone screen, and some of these apps also give you coupons scannable right from the phone.

## Lists

There's nothing wrong with using pen and paper to make lists, but some people find keeping lists on their smartphone to be more convenient. It helps them stay better organized because the phone is always at hand, so lists or notes are all in one place rather than scribbled on scraps of paper and sticky notes all around the house.

Shopping apps are perhaps the most used of list apps. You can use a grocery list app to create a checklist. As you put each item in your shopping cart, a touch of the finger on the smartphone screen checks off the item and moves it to the "purchased" section. If you frequently purchase the same items each time, you can easily uncheck the purchased items and make the list ready for the next shopping trip. No need to handwrite the same list over and over.

There are also generic list apps that let you create your own custom lists. For example, you might make a list of videos you want to see, books you have read, things to be done before a big event, items to pack for vacation, and so on. Unlike a handwritten list, completed items can be neatly deleted, keeping the list clean and easy to read until it's no longer needed.

## Ebook Reader apps

Perhaps more than any other company, Amazon is responsible for the growing popularity of ebooks. The boom in ebook reading has been caused largely by the ebook reader devices produced by Amazon (which we will discuss in a later chapter). However, in order to also make their own brand of Kindle ebooks available to people without an e-reader, Amazon has made apps to allow anyone with a computer, smartphone, or tablet to access, purchase, and read.

Sitting in front of a computer screen may not be the way most people want to read a book, and reading with the Kindle Reader app on the small screen of a smartphone may not be ideal. Still, it's nice to know these free apps are an option for those without a dedicated ebook reading device.

Free classics and public domain ebooks are available through Amazon as well as through apps created by other companies. Also, apps like Overdrive make it possible for ebook lovers to borrow selected ebooks from their local participating library—for free and from the comfort of their home.

## Audiobook app

For people who love reading but have little time, audiobooks provide an alternate way to consume books. Customers of Amazon can use the free Audible app to enjoy audiobooks and other kinds of audio content.

You can listen to audiobooks while driving, cleaning the house, exercising, knitting, or any time the mind and ears are available but the eyes and hands are occupied. Busy people who listen to audiobooks report this multitasking approach lets them enjoy a large number of books each year.

As you might have guessed, audiobooks are especially appreciated by people with limited vision, but they're equally useful to anyone with tired eyes who wants some entertainment.

Recently, Amazon has started offering selected audiobooks at a highly discounted price to people who have already purchased the ebook version of the book. Having both the ebook and audiobook means the reading experience can be synchronized, allowing the reader to easily switch back and forth between reading and listening because the apps remember the reader's place.

As with ebooks, there are apps that give audiobook listeners access to public domain works and classics in free audiobook format.

I hope this limited information about smartphones has sparked a desire to learn more. In the Resources chapter of this book, you can find more information about how to purchase a smartphone and where to look for help learning to use it.

Soon, we'll be moving into a discussion about computers (including tablet computers), but first it's necessary to talk a bit about the Internet. Smartphones come with a built-in data feature that gives you access to the Internet. Computers, on the other hand, generally can't be used for Internet access until you choose an ISP (Internet

Service Provider) and have Internet service connected to your home. Therefore, our next chapter will address the Internet and wi-fi.

# 4. THE INTERNET AND WI-FI

First, let's talk briefly and in simple terms about the meaning of "the Internet" and key words associated with it.

The Internet is a global system of computer networks that include private, public, academic, business, and government websites and documents. Because it's a web-like interconnected system of networks, the Internet is often referred to as "the web" or "the net," and locations or sites on the Internet are called "websites."

Each website on the Internet has a name or location called a URL (Uniform Resource Locator), also sometimes referred to as its "address." A URL generally has a format that looks something like this:

www.nameofwebsite.com

When you see such a URL in your browser, it usually has an underline or different color text to indicate it's an interactive link. This means when you click (or touch, in the case of a smartphone or tablet) the link, the browser will take you to that location.

To use the Internet, you'll need a high-speed connection through an ISP (Internet Service Provider). Depending on where you live and the amount of money you want to spend, you'll likely choose between a cable company, a satellite provider, a fiber provider, or a phone company that can install a DSL (digital subscriber line) connection. (Cable and DSL are the most common.) You can get information about these options by asking people in your area which they use and whether they're satisfied with their service.

If you already use a smartphone, you can search for information about options with your phone. *Yellow Pages* also have information about getting an Internet connection. Keep in mind that if you already have a Cable TV provider (such as Comcast or Time Warner), they also offer bundled plans that include an Internet connection, so it would be worthwhile to contact them to ask about the plans and prices.

The ISP brings an Internet connection from the outside into your house, and then it passes through an electronic device called a modem. It's possible to rent a modem from the provider for a small fee included in your monthly bill, or you can purchase your own from a local store that sells electronic equipment. Many people opt to rent the modem because it's convenient and guaranteed to be compatible with your provider's service.

Most mobile tech devices are connected to the Internet only by an over-the-air (wireless) connection called "wi-fi." Wi-fi is a technology using radio waves to connect computers, smartphones, and other devices to the Internet. This requires a router to convert the incoming signal from the modem to a wireless signal that your wi-fi-capable devices can recognize and use.

If this information seems overwhelming, keep in mind that there's certainly someone who would be happy to assist you in getting an Internet connection. If a neighbor, friend, or relative is unable to guide you, they almost certainly have a tech-savvy acquaintance who can.

In the rare case that you have no such option, another idea is to look in the *Yellow Pages* for a local shop that does computer and electronic device repairs. They might be available for a fee to come to your home and set up an Internet and wi-fi connection, or they might be able to refer you to someone who can.

Next, let's talk about the types of computers and what they can do. Because tablets are basically a type of touchscreen computer, the next chapter will include both computers and tablets.

# 5. COMPUTERS (AND TABLETS)

In this chapter, we'll look at basic information about how using a computer might benefit you.

There are three main types of computers—desktops, notebooks (sometimes called "laptops"), and tablets.

## Desktop Computer

A desktop computer consists of a CPU (Central Processing Unit—the "brains" of your computer where data manipulations take place), a keyboard and a mouse or trackpad that let you communicate with the computer, and a monitor with screen by which you view your input and the computer's responses.

The price of desktop computers is usually tied to how powerful they are and the complexity of work they can do as well as the quality and size of the monitor you choose.

One advantage of desktop computers is that the buyer can buy the various components separately, for example, choosing the keyboard or mouse most comfortable for them.

## Notebook Computer

A notebook computer combines the CPU, keyboard, trackpad, and screen into one integrated whole with a hinge permitting the screen to close over the keyboard like a book. The integration means the buyer loses the ability to choose components as is possible with a desktop. However, at least notebooks are available in a variety of screen dimensions and power levels (determined by the type of CPU and the amount of memory available for storing information).

As you might imagine, notebooks attract buyers because they're lightweight and portable. An internal battery makes it possible to get work done anywhere despite lack of an electrical outlet.

# Tablet Computer

Tablets have similar capabilities to other computers, and their advantages include lighter weight and portability, ease of use, and cheaper cost. Besides the tablet itself costing less than a computer, apps used on tablets are much cheaper than computer programs.

Tablets are so portable because of the "virtual" keyboard that appears on the touch-sensitive screen. It's possible to use a physical keyboard with a tablet through a wireless connection feature known as "Bluetooth," but most people find the on-screen keyboard adequate for small amounts of typing.

There are two main disadvantages of a tablet compared to a computer. Some people prefer a keyboard and mouse or trackpad instead of a touchscreen, and some prefer the larger computer screen.

Tablets and smartphones both have touchscreens and use the same kind of apps. The larger tablet screen makes it easier to use, but a smartphone is more portable and has the ability to make calls.

The operating systems of most popular tablets, as with smartphones, are either Android or iOS. If you have both a smartphone and a tablet with the same OS, you can use the same apps you have purchased on both.

Tablets sold by phone carriers are available in wi-fi-only models and wi-fi plus data plan models. Wi-fi-only tablets require you to be within range of wi-fi in order to connect to the Internet, but they save you the rather high monthly cost of a data plan. If you want to be sure you can access the Internet anytime, you need a tablet with both data and wi-fi features.

Tablets come in various screen sizes, from the size of a trade paperback book up to the equivalent of a large notebook screen. Currently, Apple's iPad tablets come in three sizes. Tablets with the Android OS come in many sizes including the most popular 7-inch format.

## Computer Operating Systems

Operating System is abbreviated as "OS." The two most common computer operating systems are Windows (Microsoft) and OS X (Apple). The Windows OS is available on desktops and notebooks manufactured by HP, Dell, Lenovo, Asus, Acer, and others. Apple's OS X is intended for use only on Apple Macintosh computers.

Both Windows and OS X have basically the same features and capabilities. Workplace computers will usually use Windows OS, but individuals purchasing their own computer can choose based on personal preference and cost.

# Software

Software is a program that tells the computer what to do. As we noted earlier, smartphones have a main operating system (iOS or Android) and also apps to do specific things. In the same way, computers have an operating system (Windows or OS X) and other software programs for specialized functions. Some programs come pre-installed and others are available from the Internet.

First, let's take a look at programs usually pre-installed on computers: the browser, email, a calendar, and contacts (an address book).

# Browser

The browser is your window to the whole Internet. The large screen size of a computer makes browser use easier and more pleasant than on mobile devices. The browser is the main way to locate and download (receive from the Internet) other programs you want to install on your computer.

The browser pre-installed on your computer may be Edge, Internet Explorer, Chrome or Safari. Others (such as Firefox) are available free on the Internet.

## Search

When you click on the browser icon, a window opens on your computer screen. On the bar at the top of the window, you'll see a small spy glass symbol indicating a search box where you type a word or phrase related to something you want to find. It might be a topic, or the name of a person or company.

The search results are a list of links leading to that information. If you already know the URL for the website you want to view, you just type it into the "address bar" at the top of the browser window.

If you're a computer novice, books are available to explain how to use browsers and other computer programs. These and other resources will be mentioned later in this book.

Next, let's take a look at just a few types of information accessible through the browser. Please keep in mind that we have already talked about using a smartphone browser, and many of the same things apply to the computer browser. The main difference is the larger computer screen makes it easier to read text and select buttons or links.

## Research

Every browser comes with a default search feature called a "search engine" such as Google, Yahoo, or Bing. It's possible to change your preferred search engine or add others to the search selection on the browser. You can search for text or images. Access to the Internet is like having a free multi-volume encyclopedia at your fingertips.

Let's examine just a few common kinds of searches.

A search for a business or company name will give you quick access to the address, phone number and a map with location and detailed driving instructions. Most businesses have either their own website or are included in one of the Internet information services that work like an online *Yellow Pages*. Each company website includes all sorts of information about their history, products, services, employment opportunities, as well as location and telephone numbers.

People often search for medical information. There are websites about various diseases, symptoms, types of treatments, traditional and alternative medicine, and the location of hospitals and medical centers.

Thanks to the Internet, people save money through DIY (Do It Yourself) projects, guided by step-by-step instructions found online.

In the Appendix of this book, you'll find a list of websites to get you started exploring the Internet.

Before we move on to the next section, let me tell you a personal story about how the Internet saved me the cost of a new pair of earphones.

After several months of heavy use, the left earphone's sound became almost inaudible. Assuming they had worn out, I was about to throw them away. Before taking that step, I did a search for information about sound problems with earphones and discovered helpful information about how to safely remove buildup of wax and dirt. In ten minutes, both the left and right earphones were sounding like new, and I didn't waste money by prematurely buying a new pair.

## Shopping

People are discovering the ease and convenience of buying things through the Internet, an activity called "online shopping."

An Internet search provides reviews of products and information about where they can be purchased. Reviews and price comparisons help you make a wise purchase and save money whether you buy online or at a local store. Also, discount coupons and free shipping are often available online. Buying bulky or heavy household supplies or food staples from the Internet saves money and makes the weekly trip to the local supermarket much easier.

Due to the low overhead costs, online sellers often offer better prices than local stores, and items not available anywhere locally are usually found somewhere online. Large online stores (such as Amazon) have almost everything imaginable along with fast shipping from regional warehouses.

The Internet helps buyers connect with individual sellers in their local area so they can purchase used items inexpensively. One example is the Craig's List website, available for every metropolitan area in the United States. Craig's List advertises services like employment opportunities and local rentals plus items for sale such as furniture, appliances, baby and kids items, books, clothes, computers, household items, antiques, musical instruments, tools, and toys and games.

In addition to shopping online for general items, there are some categories of online shopping that may be of special interest to seniors. One example is food delivery.

Some local pizza shops have had online ordering services for a long time, and other restaurants are beginning to offer this as well. Before ordering, you can view the menu (usually with photos of the offerings) and check prices for the order and delivery fee. Then, you can select items, provide your address and phone number, and enter a credit card number. Ordering food delivery online is useful when you're unable to drive to a restaurant due to health or bad weather. It's also helpful when people drop in unexpectedly and you want to have a meal together at home.

Another online delivery service is grocery delivery. Although not available in all areas, some large metropolitan supermarkets are creating an online version of their store, making available a selection of their best-selling products. If you're unable to go to the supermarket, online grocery delivery might be just what you need.

# Education

All kinds of free and paid courses are available on the Internet, making it possible to study anything from a personal hobby to a full university course. You can view video presentations at your own pace and as often as you like. Some online courses include documents to print out and keep for future reference. Some include ways to interact with other students and ask the teacher questions. If you believe in the benefits of lifelong learning, online classes are worth exploring.

# News

When you have access to the Internet, you have access to any kind of news (world, local, political, sports, celebrity, etc.) whenever you like. Many newspapers and TV stations have a website with articles and news videos. Internet news sources are especially appreciated by people who want to save money by not subscribing to cable or other paid television services.

# Banking

As you already learned from the chapter about smartphones, online banking is providing needed services. People appreciate the convenience of being able to check account balances, transfer funds between accounts, schedule bill payments, and so on.

## Entertainment

Even without cable or a similar service, there's plenty of free and inexpensive entertainment available on the Internet. As you know from the discussion of streaming video in the chapter about smartphones, websites like Hulu, YouTube, Amazon Video, and Netflix give you free or low-cost options for entertainment.

## Sports

The browser's search function will provide general information about your particular sports interest or team, and the location of your favorite team's webpage. There, you'll find schedules, ticket information, scores, stats, a player roster, news, and video clips.

## Social

People are discovering the Internet can enrich their social lives in unexpected ways. Through a topical search, you'll discover local events of interest, various kinds of support groups that meet in your area, and groups based on a common interest or hobby. These help people expand their social life and make new friends. Some have even met their spouse through such groups!

There are online social groups such as "forums" where members interact through message boards, sharing information by posting questions and comments, and replying to posts of other members. These are especially valued by people who want to find others who share some uncommon problem (like a rare disease), or wish to discuss an issue with others anonymously. They're also helpful for people without access to a local group due to their isolated location or inability to travel.

As you know from the discussion about smartphones, there are websites devoted specifically to social connections and communication such as Facebook and Twitter. These are accessible from your computer browser as well as through apps on mobile devices.

The "Groups" feature on Facebook is a good way to promote online social interaction. Facebook users are able to join or create a Group for family members, neighbors, or people with a similar interest or hobby. With the proper privacy settings, messages, photos, or videos are visible only to group members, and this helps build a close community.

## Hobbies/Interests

Through an Internet search, you can find websites, online forums, local events, and courses about almost any hobby or special interest. Just a few examples might be topics like finances, family history, pets, travel, book discussions, cooking, crafts, and retirement living. In addition to individual websites, it's possible for Facebook users to participate in a Group dedicated to such topics where people can discuss their interests and post photos.

I love to knit and crochet, so an example of one of my favorite special-interest websites is Ravelry (www.ravelry.com). Ravelry has social features like Facebook (friends, groups, and a profile page). Members can record photos and notes about each project they complete, giving them a convenient record of their work and providing comments and tips about projects that can benefit others who use the same pattern.

Ravelry also has features to help members catalog and organize information about their needles, hooks, and purchased yarn. A detailed search function lets members find a specific type of pattern among the thousands of free and paid patterns on the website.

Members can find discussion forums centered around a particular kind of project, a favorite designer, or their location, and this allows them to ask for help with a project, receive tips and advance notice about new patterns, and arrange local gatherings for members in the same area.

These are just a few examples of the useful features of a special-interest social website.

## Religious/Spiritual

People unable to attend services at their usual place of worship sometimes feel cut off from the community at a time when they need spiritual support the most. The Internet is providing some solutions to this problem.

Churches are beginning to create their own Facebook Group where members can see photos of recent events and exchange comments with others. Also, some churches broadcast their services by live streaming video or post videos for anyone to view at their convenience. Some churches make available an audio recording of the weekly sermon on their website or as a podcast.

## Helpful Information for Seniors, the Housebound or the Disabled

The Internet search function of the browser helps anyone find the information they need. However, it's an especially useful tool for locating information relevant to seniors, the housebound, or the disabled. Websites such as AARP are full of information directed toward the needs of seniors. Local government websites give details about various services available to these three groups.

Now that we have explored some of the most useful information searchable with the browser, let's turn to other computer programs: email, the photo library, the music library, live video chat, and productivity programs.

# Email

Using email on a computer is basically the same as on a smartphone except the larger computer screen makes it easier to read, and a physical keyboard or larger on-screen keyboard makes it easier to type. I've already offered suggestions in Chapter 3 about where to get an email account and how email could be useful to you.

# Photo Library

Photos taken with your smartphone camera, along with those received from others, can be edited and stored on your desktop or notebook computer. Most people who own both a smartphone and a computer transfer a copy of their photos to the computer photo library for safekeeping and backing up. In order not to lose important photos in case the computer breaks down or is stolen, people make a back-up copy to either an external storage drive that plugs into their computer or to a "Cloud" location.

The Cloud refers to a storage website on the Internet, and there are a number of Cloud services that provide space for keeping a copy of any or all of your computer contents.

Two examples of Cloud locations people use for photo storage are Flickr (www.flickr.com) and Dropbox (www.dropbox.com).

## Music Library

If you have purchased music from the Internet or copied music from CDs to your computer, it's stored in your music library. You can play music directly on your computer or connect it to a set of speakers for better sound quality. Of course, you can also connect a set of earphones or headphones to the computer if desired.

## Live Video Chat

With your computer's camera, you can enjoy free video conversations with family and friends by using a live video chat program like Skype or Google Hangouts. These services, also available as smartphone and tablet apps, are even more enjoyable on the computer screen. The image is larger, and you don't have to hold a device up to your face for the whole conversation.

These days when families live far apart, live video chats are a wonderful way to interact with grandchildren between visits.

# Productivity Programs

Some people like to use their computer for writing documents and creating spreadsheets.

Computers always come with a text editor—a basic program without many formatting features that allows users to create simple documents. Examples are Notepad (Windows) and TextEdit (OS X).

If you want to do some kind of part-time office work from your home, or a big project like writing a book, you can purchase Microsoft Word or look on the Internet for a free program with most of the same features. Apple's document creation program, Pages, comes included with their computers.

Spreadsheets are used primarily in a business setting, but if you need a spreadsheet program they're readily available. Apple computers come with the program, Numbers. Microsoft's expensive spreadsheet program, Excel, is the commercial standard. However, free options compatible with the Windows OS are available on the Internet.

This completes our overview of computers. Next up is a chapter about e-readers for you book lovers.

# 6. E-READERS

## Requirements

To purchase Amazon Kindle ebooks (and Audible audiobooks, also owned by Amazon), you must have an account with Amazon, including credit card information or gift card credits for payment. If you don't already have an Amazon account, creating one is your first step.

## Amazon Prime

Next we'll take a look at some of the features and benefits of Amazon Kindle ebooks, but first you need to be aware of a special Amazon membership program called "Amazon Prime" that is required in order to take advantage of some of the ebook perks Amazon offers.

An Amazon Prime membership costs $99 per year (at the time of this writing) and includes general benefits such as free two-day shipping for many items, Prime Video (unlimited streaming of selected free movies and TV episodes), Prime Music (unlimited, ad-free access to a large music collection), Prime Photos (secure unlimited photo storage on Amazon Cloud Drive), and Prime Pantry (discounted flat-rate delivery of selected grocery and household items).

There are two ebook-specific benefits offered under the Amazon Prime membership:

"Kindle First" gives members in the U.S. early access to a free ebook every month from the Kindle First picks (six ebooks that will be released to the public the following month).

"Kindle Owners' Lending Library" allows members in the U.S. who own an Amazon E-reader to borrow one ebook each month from a selected offering. The ebook can be kept as long as desired, but must be returned before borrowing another.

Now, let's see what Amazon Kindle ebooks offer to readers.

**Collections:** As the number of ebooks in your library increases, it's possible to organize the books into collections to make library management easier.

**Search:** The Search feature of Amazon E-readers allows you to search for a word or phrase within the book currently being read, or across all books in the library. Similarly, a search on an author's name or part of a title will bring up that content from one's own library or from matching items in the Amazon online store.

**Smart Lookup:** The Smart Lookup feature integrates a full dictionary, X-Ray, and Wikipedia (an online encyclopedia) so the reader can access definitions, characters, settings and more without leaving the page.

**Reviews:** Before purchasing an ebook, you can read details about its contents, author, length, sales rank, price, and see star ratings and reviews written by readers.

**Instant access to more ebooks:** Fans of ebooks love having instant access to purchase a new book. Without making a special trip to a bookstore or waiting for a book order to arrive by mail, readers can locate, purchase, and start reading their next book in minutes.

**Returns:** It's possible to return a purchased Kindle ebook to Amazon for a refund if you make a request within seven days of purchase.

**Borrow ebooks from your local library:** Many local libraries now make it possible for people to use their library card to borrow selected ebooks.

**Free samples:** Amazon permits customers to receive a free sample of ebooks. This usually includes the table of contents and a small percentage of the first part of the book. As with browsing a book in a bookstore, this helps the customer decide whether or not to buy a book.

**Highlighting and Notes:** As with a print book, it's possible to add highlights and notes to a Kindle ebook.

**Recommendations:** Amazon presents suggestions for other ebooks you might enjoy based on previous borrowing or purchase history. This is a convenient way to discover new books.

**Discovery by genre search:** If you're looking for a new book in a particular genre, you can enter the Kindle Store on your e-reader and explore the large number of categories and subcategories to see what is available.

**Discovery by what others purchased:** Other books you might enjoy are discoverable by looking at the details on the description page for one of your favorite books. On this page, you'll see what other books were also purchased by customers that bought this book.

**Child-friendly:** Amazon has ebooks for children and produces a Fire Kids Edition with 7-inch display, a kid-proof protective case, and a guarantee against breakage. Also, there are special security settings on all e-reader models that allow creation of a "child account" to be added to an adult's account. Because of these settings an adult is able to share their own device with a child while controlling the way the device is used and what content is accessible by the child.

**Ebook gifts:** On the description page of each ebook, there's an option for giving the ebook as a gift. The recipient receives an email notification of the gift including instructions for how to add the ebook to their Amazon Kindle Library.

**Household account:** Two adult family members with separate Amazon accounts are permitted to combine their accounts with the Household option. This allows them to share each other's ebook library, a great way to save money while expanding the number of ebooks available to both people.

**TTS (Text-to-Speech):** There's a TTS feature on Fire Tablets (not available on Kindle E-reader devices) that reads the text with an artificial voice. Although the voice sounds somewhat robotic, it can be improved by adjusting the voice speed, changing between male and female voice, and switching to a voice with a different accent. Personally, I like the female voice with a British accent. The TTS feature is great for children who can't read, people with visual limitations, or busy people who want to listen to a book while they do some other activity.

**Switch between ebook and audiobook:** If you buy an ebook that has a matching audiobook, you can purchase the audiobook at a discounted price and switch between ebook and audiobook seamlessly. The device remembers your place and picks up where you left off in either format.

**Kindle Unlimited:** If you want to borrow multiple ebooks at the same time, Kindle Unlimited may be of interest. Currently, for $9.99 per month (starting with a 30-day free trial), you can read multiple ebooks from a limited selection determined by Amazon. Kindle Unlimited works on all the free Kindle Reader apps (for iPhone and Android) as well as Amazon E-readers. This is a good way to explore new authors or genres with no risk. For the reader who seldom rereads books, a borrowing system with a monthly flat rate may make more sense than purchasing these same ebooks.

**Goodreads:** Goodreads started out as a separate website and was subsequently purchased by Amazon and integrated into their Kindle ebook services. With Goodreads, you can create personal to-read, currently reading, and read "bookshelves," rate and review books, see what friends are reading, join in discussion groups, learn more about favorite authors, and receive book recommendations based on your reviews and books you have read. Goodreads links with social networking websites like Facebook or Twitter so you can share your reading experiences with a wider audience.

Now that we've covered some of the features available on Amazon E-readers, let's talk about the two types of devices: reading-only Kindle E-reader (e-ink) devices, and multi-purpose Fire Tablet devices.

## Kindle E-readers

Kindle E-readers are dedicated devices intended only for reading ebooks. They have no sound capability and, unlike Fire Tablets, do not use apps.

Some people prefer the Kindle over the Fire Tablet because the Kindle allows them to focus on the reading experience without distractions. Compared to Fire Tablets, Kindle E-readers require less frequent battery charges, and their non-glare, paper-like, black-and-white screen is easy on the eyes and makes it possible to read outdoors in bright sunlight.

All Kindle models are approximately the size and weight of a small paperback book. Some models connect to the Internet only by wi-fi, and some are wi-fi plus free 3G. Free 3G means the device can access the Internet directly at no cost through the same radio towers that provide voice services to mobile phones.

If you have access to wi-fi at home and other places you go regularly, you don't need 3G. However, people without home wi-fi, or frequent travelers, will probably want to buy a 3G-capable device.

At the time of this writing there are three Kindle E-reader models:

- The **Kindle** is the cheapest model. There's no built-in light, so you can't use it in a dark room without an external light. It connects with the Internet only by wi-fi.

- The **Kindle Paperwhite** is the mid-price model. It has a built-in light. It's available in wi-fi only and wi-fi plus free 3G.

- The **Kindle Voyage** is the most expensive model. It has a built-in self-adjusting light. The Voyage's PagePress sensors allow the user to turn pages without lifting a finger by pressing on the bezel. Because the Voyage has a texturized screen with the highest resolution of the Kindle line, the reading experience is most like reading print on paper. The Voyage comes in wi-fi and wi-fi plus free 3G versions.

## Fire Tablets

Some people prefer a Fire Tablet over a Kindle E-reader for its color screen, range of sizes, and tablet features that make it a multi-function device.

Like any tablet, the Fire Tablet has sound (via a 3.5mm headphone jack for inserting earphones, and mono or stereo speakers depending on the model). This means the TTS feature can be used with ebooks, and the Fire Tablet can play audiobooks, music, and videos.

All models have front-facing and rear-facing cameras for taking photos, recording video, and doing live video chat with apps like Skype. Also, as with any tablet, basic apps such as browser, email, calendar, and contacts come pre-installed. Additional free and paid apps are available in Amazon's Appstore on the device.

The Fire Tablet's color screen may be difficult to read in bright sunlight due to glare, but the fact that it's always backlit means an external light is never needed.

The Fire Tablet comes in more sizes than the Kindle E-reader, and there are four models at the time of this writing. Unlike the Kindle E-reader line, Fire Tablets only connect with the Internet through wi-fi. There are no 3G options, so Fire Tablet buyers will definitely need home wi-fi and access to wi-fi when they travel.

The four Fire Tablet models are:

- **Fire HD6** with a high-definition 6-inch screen and a mono speaker.

- **Fire** (Amazon's newest and cheapest Fire Tablet.) It has a 7-inch screen (without high-definition) and a mono speaker. Fire users can insert a microSD card to increase the very small storage capacity of the device.

  The Fire comes in a special "Fire Kids Edition" that includes a Kid-Proof Case and a 2-year worry-free guarantee to replace a broken device for free—no questions asked. There are parental control settings that let parents manage usage limits, content access, and educational goals.

- **Fire HD8** with a high-definition 8-inch screen and stereo speakers.

- **Fire HD10** with a high-definition 10.1-inch screen and stereo speakers.

I hope this overview of Amazon E-readers has given you some good ideas about how your reading experience might be enriched by supplementing or replacing print books with an e-reader. To set up an Amazon account and see complete details about the devices mentioned above, use your smartphone, computer, or tablet to go to www.amazon.com.

# 7. RESOURCES

Now that you have had an overview of some devices and their benefits, you're likely feeling a bit more confident. This chapter will help you transition from tech-curious to tech-smart.

What you need at this point are resources, so we'll discuss offline and online resources next. These will help you prepare for the process of purchasing and learning to use your new tech device.

## Offline Purchasing Resources

If you're ready to purchase your first tech device, your best resource is your local circle of family, friends, and their acquaintances. (From now on, I'll refer to this group as "your network.") If they own and use the kind of device you intend to buy, ask them if they would recommend the same model for you.

People who own and use tech devices love to talk about their device, praising its strong points and complaining about its weaknesses. They can tell you where they purchased it, and they might be able to share with you information they gained during their purchase process concerning which other models are recommended and which should be avoided.

In the course of this search process, you might find that a tech-savvy friend or relative is getting ready to upgrade to a newer model and would be happy to give you their old device or sell it to you for a bargain price. Used devices that are still fairly new work just fine and are a great way to save money. In addition, the previous owner will be your natural choice when it comes to asking for tips about how to use the device.

Another suggestion for pre-purchase research is publications. Check a local store for magazines with articles and reviews about the kind of device you want to buy. Sales flyers that come in your mail or with your newspaper are another helpful resource for learning which local stores are selling devices and how much they cost.

Finally, a visit to a local store lets you see and handle devices and ask the salesperson some questions. Your local phone carrier of choice will have a display of available Apple and Android smartphones and tablets, and a local Apple Store will have iPhones, iPads, and computers. You can find some e-readers as well as smartphones, tablets, and computers at stores like Walmart and Best Buy.

# Offline Learning Resources

## At-home Teacher

Especially if this is your first tech device, an at-home teacher or mentor is the most comfortable way to learn. The first place to look is your network. There's likely to be someone willing to help you get started with your new device. They might offer to do this for free, or for a small payment, or perhaps you have something you could trade them for their time—a hand knit scarf, some freshly baked bread, a home cooked meal or whatever your special talent. If an at-home teacher is not available through your network, a phone call to a local computer repair shop might yield some leads.

# Group Instruction

Another option for learning how to use your new device is group instruction outside your home. While one-to-one help in your own home is convenient, being with other people that are interested in learning the same thing can be an enjoyable experience and a great way to make new friends with a common interest.

Let's explore some resources for group instruction.

Call local colleges to see if they offer any continuing education or lifelong learning classes that teach what you want to learn. Local libraries sometimes offer classes, so check with them, too. A community center, senior center, or YMCA in your town may offer or know of a suitable class.

If there's a Macintosh User Group in your area, it would be an excellent place to meet other users of Apple devices and ask advice about classes or one-to-one instruction.

If all of the above suggestions fail to produce results, there's one other option. If you know of a few others in your social circle that also want to learn how to use a particular kind of device, you could form your own class and hire a teacher. You could meet in a group member's home or at a public facility like a library, social center, or church.

## Books

Your local bookstore is a resource for how-to books for various devices. If there's no possibility of one-to-one instruction or a group class, a how-to book can become your teacher.

How-to books are also useful references to help you remember what you learned from a mentor or class and to supplement those lessons. I'll list a few suggestions of books you might find helpful below. You'll notice that many are part of the "for dummies" series, books known for their friendly step-by-step approach. I'll include selected books from this series written specifically with seniors in mind, but there are others on a variety of topics addressed to anyone who wants to learn something new.

*"Is This Thing On?": A Friendly Guide to Everything Digital for Newbies, Technophobes,*

*and the Kicking & Screaming* by Abby Stokes [This is the book I would recommend as a general how-to instruction manual.]

*My iPhone for Seniors (Covers iOS 9 for iPhone 6s/6s Plus, 6/6 Plus, 5s/5C/5, and 4s) (2nd Edition)* by Brad Miser

*My Windows 10 Computer for Seniors (includes Video and Content Update Program)* by Michael Miller

*Mac OS X El Capitan for Seniors: Learn Step by Step How to Work with Mac OS X El Capitan (Computer Books for Seniors series)* by Studio Visual Steps

*My iPad for Seniors (Covers iOS 9 for iPad Pro, all models of iPad Air and iPad mini, iPad 3rd/4th generation, and iPad 2) (3rd Edition)* by Gary Rosenzweig and Gary Eugene Jones

*My Facebook for Seniors (2nd Edition)* by Michael Miller

*iPad For Seniors For Dummies* by Nancy C. Muir

*iPhone for Seniors For Dummies* by Nancy C. Muir

*Windows 10 For Seniors For Dummies* by Peter Weverka

L*aptops For Seniors For Dummies* by Nancy C. Muir

*Facebook and Twitter For Seniors For Dummies* by Marsha Collier

*Computers For Seniors For Dummies* by Nancy C. Muir

*Macs For Seniors For Dummies* by Mark L. Chambers

If you already have a smartphone and are researching another tech device, you'll be able to take advantage of the phone's browser to search for information for yourself. If you're researching your first device purchase, perhaps someone in your network can help you with the Internet searches suggested in the next section.

# Online Purchasing Resources

On the Internet, there's information about all kinds of devices, their features, prices, and where to buy both locally and via online shopping.

If you're in the market for a smartphone, a browser search for the website of any phone carrier will provide information about their signal coverage for your area, the phone models they sell and their prices, the various contracts or plans they offer, and much more.

A discussion of online shopping wouldn't be complete without information about Amazon. From the chapter about e-readers, you already know Amazon is the biggest source of ebooks and ebook reading devices. In addition to these items, Amazon is a one-stop shopping solution for how-to books about technology (both ebook and print books), tech device feature and price comparisons, and reviews.

Websites like Amazon are convenient for gathering information in the comfort of your own home in order to narrow down your choices.

Then, you can purchase directly from an online store, like Amazon, or at a local store.

One other benefit of shopping online at Amazon is the new and used items from other companies and individuals available for purchase on the site. This is one more way to save money with online shopping.

If you're interested in an Amazon E-reader, the best place to buy one is directly from Amazon's online store (www.amazon.com) with free and fast shipping to your home. However, it may be possible to find some models at a Big Box store if online shopping is not possible.

A browser search for the website of Big Box stores will give you information about all of the tech devices they sell through their Internet store, making it possible to comparison shop and learn about prices and features of the devices. Take a look at Walmart (www.walmart.com) and Best Buy (www.bestbuy.com).

One option to check into with an online search is refurbished devices. These are sometimes offered directly from the original manufacturer, and also from websites that specialize in buying and selling used devices. Refurbished devices may come with a one-year warranty and are every bit as good as a new device at a fraction of the cost.

Some examples of websites that buy and sell used devices are: Swappa (www.swappa.com), Gazelle (www.gazelle.com), and Glyde (www.glyde.com).

It's possible to find Apple products at some Big Box stores, and there are physical Apple Stores in large cities. If you need to handle and try out an Apple computer, iPad, or iPhone, these are your best choice. However, if you prefer the convenience of online shopping, you can go directly to Apple's online store (www.apple.com).

In addition to new devices, there's a section on Apple's online store with a listing of currently available refurbished and clearance devices that come complete with warranty (www.apple.com/shop/browse/home/specialdeals).

Websites like Craig's List (www.craigslist.org) and eBay (www.ebay.com) are another place to check for used tech devices sold by individuals.

# Online Learning Resources

## Searching

Now that you're able to access the Internet for yourself or with help from your network, you have many more resources available to help you make purchasing decisions about other tech devices or to locate classes. By a search for a word or phrase, you can learn about device models, price comparisons, and reviews before purchasing as well as locate online stores.

You can also access the websites of local businesses, schools, senior and community centers, and libraries to see if they offer any tech classes. Searches will also bring up links to websites specializing in how-to information, articles, and help sections with answers to commonly asked questions.

## Online Articles

When you do a general search using your browser, the resulting list will contain the location of websites with products and services. You'll also see links to articles on websites devoted to seniors such as AARP (www.aarp.org) or websites like The Huffington Post (www.huffingtonpost.com/news/seniors-and-technology/) that regularly publish technology articles relevant to seniors.

Blogs (web logs) are also a good source of articles on various topics. Blogs are websites run by individuals or businesses where information and opinion articles are posted regularly.

When you locate a website with lots of useful information, you can remember it with the bookmark feature of your browser and revisit the site easily.

## Online Forums

An online forum is an interactive message board. People write comments or questions, and others respond with further comments or answers. Some websites include a Forum section and also a Help section or FAQ (Frequently Asked Questions) section that may be helpful to you.

## YouTube

YouTube is a good place to find lots of free videos about devices and how-to information. For the tech device online shopper, YouTube has "unboxing" videos where people record the opening of the package containing their newly received tech device while describing their first impressions. Even more in-depth review videos are available, as well as how-to videos about using the device.

## Educational Websites

Good free and paid how-to instructional courses are offered on the Internet. They're intended for anyone wanting to take advantage of online education, but a few are directed specifically at the needs of seniors. Here are a few examples of both types:

Lynda (www.lynda.com)

Udemy (www.udemy.com)

ScreenCastsOnline
(www.screencastsonline.com) The focus is on Apple products.

Ask Abby (www.askabbystokes.com) The website of Abby Stokes, author of the book *"Is This Thing On?": A Friendly Guide to Everything Digital for Newbies, Technophobes, and the*

*Kicking & Screaming.* Here, you'll find tutorials, videos, and supplemental material for her book.

Techboomers (www.techboomers.com). As the name suggests, Techboomers is a website created especially to help seniors become familiar with commonly used websites, Internet services, and apps. Techboomers does a nice job with basic articles complete with pictures and diagrams.

The offline and online resources covered in this section are just a few examples to get you started. Most people find that as they start to explore these resources, they discover other resources leading to even more.

You have become tech-smart by exploring your own thinking, the devices you might enjoy, and the resources available to help you get started. You know so much more than you did when we set off on this journey, and this is just the beginning. However, the last and most important step is in the next chapter.

# 8. TECH-ACTIVE!

Our journey together is drawing to a close. When we first met, you were tech-timid, but willing to face your fear and self-doubt.

Gradually, you began to defeat the little voice in your head and your inclination to remain in your comfort ("stuck") zone. You moved from tech-timid to tech-curious as we explored some wonderful devices, and you let yourself start dreaming about their benefits.

Now, with added information about practical resources, you have transitioned from tech-curious to tech-smart.

One more step is needed, and it's perhaps the most important step of all—Take action!

Let me explain why taking action is so important.

When I became a senior, I became more aware of the issues seniors face. Now I look at my own situation and that of seniors in my social circle and community. I read articles about physical, mental, and emotional challenges that commonly come with the aging process and cause a narrowing of the world for seniors.

I learn that many seniors face physical problems such as declining strength, failing eyesight, loss of agility, and forgetfulness.

These problems, in turn, lead to some loss of independence as a result of no longer being able to drive or facing the need to downsize and move to a location providing more senior services. This may mean being cut off from easy access to longtime friends that have become an important part of their social support system. The death of peers in their social circle causes an additional narrowing of their world.

Perhaps you're not currently facing these issues, but a friend or family member may be, and you're likely to face some of them in the future.

When your world begins to narrow in this way, it's natural to feel helpless to do anything about it.

You're retired and no longer have the daily challenge of the work and the stimulation of interacting with coworkers. Your social circle seems to be ever shrinking, you can only do so much to try to stay healthy, and you no longer drive at night (or at all). When you do have opportunities to spend time with younger people, their topics of conversation and interests seem foreign and irrelevant to you.

You begin to feel increasingly isolated, bored, lonely, negative, and perhaps even depressed. You try to fill your time with watching the same old television programs, reading the newspaper, and playing solitaire. You start to wonder if life is passing you by, and perhaps you begin to feel decreasing hope for the future.

It's true that you can't make these problems and challenges just go away, and even those you can combat take some time and effort before you see results. But there *is* hope and there are some things you *can* do to fight the boredom and loneliness, exercise your brain, find new opportunities, and make new friends of all ages. In short, you *can* expand your world.

I face many of the problems and issues mentioned above, and yet my life feels full and interesting. Why? A commitment to lifelong learning.

Throughout my life, I've made a commitment to myself to always be learning and trying new things. To my great relief and joy, I've found I can use technology to continue expanding my world despite limitations that come with aging.

The Internet and the tech devices I own have put the whole world at my fingertips. I often think my life wouldn't be nearly as rich without them, and that's why I'm so eager to share my love of technology with other seniors like you—eager enough to write a book!

So, you have reached the point in your journey where you face the final step—action.

Here, as always, you have a choice—action or regrets.

If you don't take action, you can retreat back into your familiar comfort zone and try to forget what you've learned from this book. Your life will not change and your world will not expand. At some point in the future, you'll likely come to regret this choice.

If you do take action, your courage, self-confidence and sense of satisfaction will grow, and your life will be enriched. I've never yet met anyone that took action and regretted it.

Let me tell you my own recent experience with beginning a new journey and facing the "take action" step.

This year I decided to open myself up to something totally new—writing a book for the first time. I experienced all the same things we've discussed: self-doubt, fear, feeling overwhelmed, and not knowing where to start. I followed the advice I'm going to give you here and the result is the book you're now reading.

The secret to overcoming my fear and "stuck" feelings was to face my fear and then create an action plan.

I had to acknowledge my fear and question the underlying beliefs (as we did in Chapter 1). I didn't ignore or deny the fear, but I chose not to let it control or stop me. I reminded myself that the act of taking action is one of the best ways to conquer fear, and that fear usually subsides with each action step taken. I also reminded myself that the purpose of an action plan is to avoid the overwhelmed feeling preventing the taking of the first step.

My action plan started with locating an online course to guide me in the book writing process. All the steps needed to complete the project were listed and put in order. By methodically taking each step one after the other, I reached the end of the process. Through the experience, I learned a lot of things about myself, found a wonderful community of authors, made new friends, attained a new level of self-confidence and joy, and learned new skills that may open other doors in the future.

Was the process easy? No, it required a lot of hard work and self-discipline. Was the process as difficult as I feared? Not at all. By taking the first steps, the fear and overwhelmed feelings subsided and the sense of satisfaction and accomplishment grew.

I'm glad I didn't let fear keep me prisoner in my comfort ("stuck") zone. I'm glad I'm not going to find myself looking back with regret and wondering what might have been. And, most of all, I'm excited that I now have this book to share with you.

Well, that's my story. Now it's your turn.

- Face your fear and tell it who's boss.

- Remind yourself that you've already successfully made the journey from tech-timid to tech-curious to tech-smart.

- Make your action plan. (Write down all the small steps needed to take action on the information in this book and put them in order.)

- Take the first step.

- Do it now!

# THE TECH-ACTIVE WORLD IS ONLY ONE STEP AWAY!

# APPENDIX

## HEALTH

PubMed (www.ncbi.nlm.nih.gov/pubmed/)
Medscape (www.medscape.com)
WebMD (www.webmd.com)

## HOBBIES & SPECIAL INTERESTS

Ancestry (www.ancestry.com)
Cooking (www.epicurious.com)
Knitting (www.ravelry.com)

## NEWSPAPERS & MAGAZINES

USA Today Online (www.usatoday.com)
Wired Magazine (www.wired.com)
The New Yorker Magazine
        (www.newyorker.com)
People Magazine (www.people.com)
TV Guide (www.tvguide.com)

The Washington Post
(www.washingtonpost.com)

# RESEARCH

White Pages Online (www.whitepages.com)
Refdesk (www.refdesk.com)

# SENIORS

Senior Planet (www.seniorplanet.org)
Social Security Administration (www.ssa.gov)
Third Age (www.thirdage.com)
AARP (www.aarp.org)

# SHOPPING

Home Depot (www.homedepot.com)
Macy's (www.macys.com)
Peapod (www.peapod.com)
Shaw's (www.shaws.com)
Consumer Reports
(www.consumerreports.org)
Shopzilla (www.shopzilla.com)
Freecycle (www.freecycle.org)

# SPORTS & ENTERTAINMENT

ESPN (www.espn.com)
IMDb (www.imdb.com)

# TRAVEL

Expedia (www.expedia.com)
Hotels (www.hotels.com)
Lonely Planet (www.lonelyplanet.com)
Trip Advisor (www.tripadvisor.com)
Kayak (www.kayak.com)

# ACKNOWLEDGMENTS

A huge "Thank You!" to the following people
without whom this book would not have
become a reality

My sister, Kay Ling
for being an inspiration and a sounding board
(and the "bestest" sister ever)

My SPS Coach, Jaime Grodberg
for providing guidance and encouragement

My "Book Buddy," Doug Buettner
for keeping me accountable through the
process

My cover designer, Heidi Sutherlin
for sharing her unique creative flair

My formatter, Debbie Lum
for her great work making this book readable

My Launch Team,
for all their help in introducing this book to the
world

# ABOUT THE AUTHOR

Thanks to a librarian aunt and parents who passed on their love of reading, Marie spent much of her childhood with her nose in a book. Her love of learning, and sharing what she learns, lead to a 16-year career teaching English in Japan.

Living in another country prompted Marie to learn about technologies that would keep her in touch with family and friends. She learned about email, IM, and Skype and in the process discovered the amazing wealth of information available on the Internet.

Now retired and living in New Hampshire, Marie still has a passion for learning and technology. She finds her life enriched by podcasts and audiobooks, ebooks, language learning resources, streaming video, online shopping, Facebook, Ravelry (an online community of knitters), and researching anything and everything.

Marie's current mission is to share the joys and benefits of technology with other seniors. In her book *Become a Tech-Active Senior*, she helps seniors work through mental and emotional barriers standing in the way of embracing a tech-rich life, and presents basic information about useful tech devices that match the needs and interests of seniors.

Marie can be contacted at
mclapsaddle.author@gmail.com.

# May I ask a favor?

If this book has been useful to you, please consider leaving a review on Amazon. Reviews are very important because they help other readers discover good books, and they are a big encouragement to the author.

Thank you!

~ Marie Clapsaddle

Made in the USA
Lexington, KY
27 April 2018